SOUL FRIENDS

A Selection of Inspirational Verses

SOUL FRIENDS

A Selection of Inspirational Verses

by

ANNETTE BORRILL

Date of Publication:
2001

Published by:
W M A Books Ltd
Willow Lodge
Old Leake
Boston
Lincolnshire
PE22 9QY

Printed by:
ProPrint
Riverside Cottage
Great North Road
Stibbington
Peterborough PE8 6LR

ISBN: 0 9541705 0 4

CONTENTS

ACKNOWLEDGEMENTS

Special thanks to Sheila, for believing in me and enabling me to develop my writing, also my other soul friends: Shirley, Eileen, Doreen, Graham, Edna, Sue, Trina, Eliza, Margery, Rosemary, The Temple Family, Anne, Jim, Lorraine and family in England and Ireland.

Although I can't mention everyone by name, my thoughts go to many others, especially in the villages of Wrangle and Stickney . . . Many thanks to the women I have met through my work and to those who, although no longer physically here, remain my 'soul' friends, including my late Headmaster, Mr F J Barrand, who encouraged me so much, Kath, Beryl and my late family. Finally thanks to Chris' for his computer expertise.

FOREWORD

Over the years I have met many people who have inspired me; they are the gentle people, with laughter and compassion in their eyes. I have also experienced the pain of rejection, from those with eyes of steel.

Perhaps, like me, you are happy to trust that you are travelling along the path you were destined to tread. Perhaps, also like me, there are times in life when you need to feel 'held' and understood. If so I hope you will find comfort in this little book. A few quiet moments amidst the turmoil of life can enable us to reconnect with our inner-self and allow our angels to reach us! Before you open the book, close your eyes, sit quietly and see which page you are drawn to . . .

Life is a complicated business! Perhaps it is time to return to the simple philosophy of my late grandfather: make the most of what you have, stay enthusiastic, look for the good in those you meet - rather than look to criticise, laugh *with* others - not *at* them, offer a helping hand and most of all ENJOY life! Surrounded by difficulties he was always at peace with himself and the world; he held beauty within his heart and for those who knew him the world was a special place.

I understand the old Gaelic term for love and friendship is 'anam ̇cara', meaning soul friend; hence the title 'Soul Friends'.

May the light of your soul offer guidance and your guardian angels bring you peace, love and a little laughter!

DEDICATION

I would like to dedicate this book of inspirational verses to my family; especially my late mother, Mona, and my late grandfather, Bill, in remembrance of their love for the written word and artistic gifts - but especially for the love, sensitivity, laughter and inspiration they shared with me throughout their lives.

ANGELIC MESSAGES

I thought I caught a glimpse
of an angel passing by.
I'm sure I saw a figure
of gold within the sky.
I know I heard a message
somewhere inside my head.
'Go quietly, trust and
be at peace, you're loved,'
the message said.

Perhaps the breeze misled me;
perhaps the golden light
I felt run through my weary soul
was merely just sun-light
- making me feel whole.
Or maybe I was right first time,
an angel came to me
and held me tight in sweet embrace
and whispered, 'Peace; be free.

Let no-one take your sweetness
and turn it into spite;
let no one take your gift of hope,
or turn you from the light.
And if at times you're downcast
and joy is hard to see,
just look above
with loving heart
and catch a glimpse of me . . .'

LOOK FOR JOY

In quiet moments peace spreads her wings
- sends gratitude for gentle things,
encourages us to put life first;
to look for joy, not think the worst!
And Nature reaches out to say
relax, ENJOY this perfect day.
Embrace your friends
and kind thoughts send
- perhaps today a friendship mend . . .

Forget the stress of yesterday;
forget the need to have your say.
Just do your best to put things right
by understanding and you just might
find a happier way to live
- by sharing all you have to give.
There may be little hope around
then deep within God's love is found
- soon joy and smiles once more surround . . .

FATE

Yesterday it stayed with us
listening to our sighs,
demanding we be bold.

Today it gently holds us
listening to our 'How's?'
'With patience' we are told.

Tomorrow we must learn to trust
and with life's rhythm flow.
Fate will always guide us
- but first we must 'let go' . . .

And when we finally understand
that this has worked for years.
We'll feel relief and simply let
Fate wipe away our tears.

Fate will take us safely forward
in arms of blue and gold.
Enlightened, encircled, loving -
towards our Spirit's goal.

TERESA

Peat warms the hearth
within a grate of lead.
Warmth surrounds the family there,
Irish eyes so full of life
- arms that hug and care!

A SPECIAL THOUGHT

Useless anger;
joyless world,
imposing will
of steel?

Helpful words;
a happy life,
support to help
you heal?

'Making choices';
simply said,
not so simply done,
you feel?

Using gifts;
creating love
as on your knees
you kneel . . .

Using prayer;
your inner - strength
begins to break
the seal.

A special thought
comes to your mind;
God's guidance;
loving, real . . .

LET TIME PASS

Feel fear depart
Listen music ~ sing!
Open your heart
Allow life to loving
The longed for new start!

THE HAPPY ME

The Happy Me
is a golden thread,
woven through body and soul,
always linked to the Universe;
it keeps me safe and whole!

JUDGING

Do we judge by appearance
- by colour, age or creed?

Do we judge by what is said
- or by a person's deed?

Do we judge by wealth
or a poor man by his clothes?

Do we judge by who knows what
- or how a person grows?

Do we judge by comments made
by friends when they may call?

Do we judge?
Must we judge?

Wouldn't life be better -
if we didn't 'judge' at all?

JUST BILL

'Think positive' the experts say,
and we all try from day to day.
But now and then someone appears,
who does it naturally through the years!

Bill always smiled; Bill always helped
a neighbour when he could.
Bill always gave and never took -
believed in all - just looked for good!

He was the dearest person
that there could ever be.
He was just 'Bill' to everyone -
but Grandad Bill to me!

JUST

Just one word - the loving kind -
enables us to leave behind
the pain we sometimes feel
Just a thoughtful, cheery card
can help us start to heal . . .

Just a smile can reassure
the inner-part of you.
Just one hug to say, 'I care'
is so important too!

Just a face - a friendly face -
can make our world a better place.
Just a prayer - a tiny prayer -
will comfort us
for He is there . . .

THE BUD OF LIFE

Tonight as I sat thinking
of how it used to be,
I pictured family outings
- a cottage by the sea.
I saw somebody running
towards two loving hands;
I realised the child was me
running through the sands . . .

And 'though those loving hands have gone
and there is only me
I know that love still reaches out
from way beyond the sea.
I cannot *see* that far away
- sometimes I wish I could!
But somewhere hidden deep inside
I know *this* life is just the bud . . .

MOONDREAMS AND SUNBEAMS

Moondreams and Sunbeams dance
in my secret scheme.
Fairies, safe from harsh reality,
flit and take their chance
to dream by winding stream.

The sweetness of a bygone age
fills the air once more.
Sunbeams and moonbeams speak of love
as we walk along the shore.

Lonely tears may mingle
with tears of happiness.
Rainbows and Sunshine,
within the winds of time,
cloak my emptiness.

Moondreams and Sunbeams dance
in my secret scheme.
Respite from today's reality;
allowing mind and soul
to join silently together
gentle, peaceful - whole . . .

THE LAKE

Lyrical sounds of a magic flute
allaying fear.
Hushed content;
my soul at rest
whenever water's near . . .

UNIVERSAL LOVE

Alone I stand on deserted beach
- water stretching from my reach
to a world beyond . . .

Alone I stand;
my fear now gone.
The Universe and I are one.

JUST ANOTHER STREAM

Meandering it leads me
to where I want to be
sometimes silent, sometimes flowing
- reminding me, *I'm Free!*

WELCOME

God comes when you invite him,
a very welcome guest.
So why not say a little prayer
that he will grant you rest . . .

DOWN DAYS

If life has made you weary
- you're tired of doing your best -
just 'let go' for a little while
and let your life be blessed.

THE THIEF

When pain intrudes
as it likes to do!
Remind yourself
that you're still 'you' . . .

ANGER!

Take a deep breath
and on its release
let go of the anger
that makes foreheads crease!

CANDLES AND CRYSTALS

Do you ever light a candle
and feel the peace it brings?

Have you ever held a crystal
and felt its magic healing things?

Will you spend a little time
- just an hour, or minute?

To close your eyes and say a prayer.
- there's so much love within it!

Even in silence, guidance is there
- especially in silence, God hears our prayer.

Though life may bombard us
with noise, rush and stress . . .

In quiet moments
our Lord will still Bless.

THE HUMBLE WREN

Oh gentle wren you swiftly fly
to secret places
from the sky.
Darting here and darting there;
quickly, quickly, everywhere.
And if a stalking cat should peer
round the corner
- very near -
you shout so loud;
machine - gun sound,
on and on
- fly round and round!
Your warning seems to take effect,
the cat sits still, 'though quite erect.
Your little mission's now complete
- the cat retreats beneath the seat!

THE STRUTTER AND THE STROLLER

As you take your walk through life
the pace is up to you.
Do you want to march along -
or take a stroll or two?

Do you want to strut with pride,
or do you want to plod?
Do you want to trudge alone -
or walk along with God?

Do you want to shuffle -
to stagger, reel and lurch?
Or do you want to wander -
just amble in your search?

Perhaps you want to change the pace,
or go a different way . . .
The choice is yours; the path is yours.
Remember this each day!

LIFE IS A RAINBOW

Moonlit shadows on silver pond;
meandering streams creating a bond
with grasses and creatures there.
A mare and foal; the fox in her lair,
Destiny's fingers touching each hare.

Violets, shyly peeping from hedges;
bold, bright flowers competing on ledges.
Tiny mice, alert with fear,
dart away, whilst grazing deer
greet another dawn.

Bird-songs of freedom vibrantly bring
new life; new hope, on the first day of spring.
Hedges of brown, with hints of green hue
sit silently watching, heavy with dew,
protecting and shielding the fledglings so new.

Misty meadows; portraits of green -
bewitching, beguiling - creating a scene
o'er woodland, fen and lane,
basking in sunshine and welcoming rain.
Nature quietly displays once again . . .

A rainbow of smiles - tinged with tears -
throughout the seasons; throughout the years.
Long summer days and long winter nights,
fate's hand unfolding beyond these sights,
caressing my face and calming my fears.

WOMEN NEED . . .

Women need love and laughter,
although it often seems,
life throws prickly branches
instead of perfect dreams . . .

Women need a loving touch,
although it often seems,
life throws cold hostility
that wounds a soul so much . . .

Women need a listening ear,
although it often seems,
life throws impatient glances,
and no one listens fear . . .

Women need to know they're loved
although it often seems,
they are put upon this earth
to fulfil another's dreams!

REAL LOVE

Real love is a generous spirit.
Real love embraces pain.
Real love is unconditional.
Real love keeps you sane.

MAGICAL MAY

Wispy spirits weaving spells
o-er woodland, grove and stream.
Enigmatic fairy rings,
where woodland folklore breathes
and whispers Nature's dream . . .

Halcyon, dove-like spirits charm
flowers into bloom.
Covertly, quietly, magically, aromatic balm
is woven by the loom
of life . . .

Fragility's fragrance, essence of pure white light,
captured in the moment on water in the night.
Impressions on a willow's leaves, a charismatic sigh,
as in the world of tranquillity
an angel passes by . . .

MEDITATE

Huffing and puffing, face quite red,
yelling and screaming, kids sent to bed.
Stretching and sighing, face quite serene,
quietly picturing your own tranquil scene . . .

A TRUE GEM

A rose window of dreams;
fleur-de-lis
woven into a soul.
Fine tapestry; uncut jewels
- sapphire, turquoise and gold.

Embellished, intricate pattern
interlaced with love and fear.
A choker, a chain or a crucifix?
Uncut gem; precious amulet
- protection through the year . . .

Moonstone, vividescent emerald,
sea of apple and midnight blue.
A kaleidoscope of colour
- diverse jewels -
make the Being that is 'You'.

PEACE

If the new beginning's ended
and there's turmoil all around.
Look to the light and say a prayer,
for peace can still be found . . .

SEEDS OF JOY

A parachute of stars
illuminate the earth,
translucent vision of crystal clear light;
serenity's birth.

Rainbow colours; pure white light
extinguish the darkness of the night.
Sunshine smiles from sunlit souls
sprinkle magic on jet black coals.

Disillusioned spirits can once more sing
as a flame of life the black coals bring.
And in the bowels of the earth
seeds of joy prepare for birth . . .

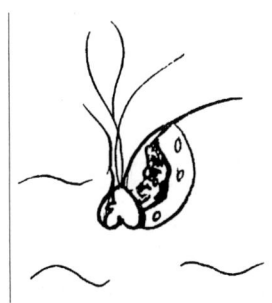

NIGHTFALL

Snow driven, ivory life pad;
swan on silver throne.
A silver frosted lake.

White hot candles fade.
The blackbird sings no more
in toffee burnt-almond glade.

Sunflower apricot sunsets gone;
no marmalade sky
or coppery beech nearby.

No reflection on rippling stream
just leaden skies.
Twilight; owl-light greyness.
Night falls; silhouettes dance.
A starless sky sleeps.
Heaven's blind gives rest a chance!

BELIEVE IN YOURSELF

Confidence is positive; arrogance offends.
Humour lightens many lives -
no matter what the trends!
Love, the unconditional kind,
reassures the heart and mind.
Kindness calms the troubled soul
but self-acceptance makes us whole!

INNER STRENGTH

When loneliness echoes
and misery beckons
with finger of icy steel.

When people torment
and trivialise
all that you think is real.

When you need someone
to come to you
and they walk away instead.

When all seems lost
and cares mount up
forget what's in your head.

Look to the place within yourself
that no one else can reach
. . . and let your spirit speak . . .

THE WORLD BEYOND

Surrounded by memories she sits alone;
photographs, letters, a keepsake - no 'phone.
A chair by the window, her link with the world;
or maybe a broken chain?

In her mind's eye she sees visitors at the door,
smiling, laughing, like years before.
Her mind is a cloud; heavy with pain.

Now quietly crying she tries to be strong,
scolds herself softly and wonders how long
it will be before someone remembers she's there . . .

She puts on her coat, wears socks that don't match,
walks to the door and lifts the old latch.
The snow-covered path with its uneven ground,
brings her falling, falling - no one's around . . .

A bright light so dazzling she cannot believe,
envelops her spirit, she quietly leaves
a cold world behind.

No sadness, no regret - a new life unfurled
completely at peace in a beautiful world.
Reality.

ANGEL OF THE NIGHT

At depth of night
when rest won't come
and minutes seem like hours;
when painful thoughts
won't leave your mind
and loneliness
shows off its powers.
Just take a breath,
release a sigh
and know an angel
passing by
will always be with you.

ROOTS AND THE LIGHT

Roots in the ground
when surrounded by negativity,
like the seed in heavy soil,
wait -
but also push upwards
towards the light.

Don't lie dormant
submerged in the darkness.
Allow the natural process
to guide you in your growth
- return to clear thought and vision
through determination and prayer,
as you push upwards
- towards the light!

HOPE

Hope is a sanctuary within,
awaiting our call;
longing to awaken
new joy inside us all!

BE GENTLE

How brave to be gentle
in a world that respects the strong -
where gentleness is seen as weak,
by those who've got it wrong!

ANGELIC LOVE

When muddy waters of misery
fill your mind
and tears spill
fountains of fear
you'll find
loving angels
gather round
and help
until peace
can be
found . . .

THE TREACHEROUS EAR

Envious people 'hear' of us
what they choose to believe is true.
It rarely bears resemblance
to the Being that is you!
In their mind's eye and thorny gaze
it seems somehow they must erase
all that makes us dance.
And in its place leave misery -
if we let them have the chance!

LOVE

L ike yourself when life's unfair:
O ffer your hand and say a prayer.
V ery often (it's nothing rare)
E nlightened Beings will show they care!

FIZZY LOLLIES AND HOLLOW EGGS

Cuckoo flowers crept down the slope
which led to the stream beyond.
A tiny, homely cottage sat quietly by the pond
in which tadpoles lived in hope
of turning into frogs, thanks to life's magic wand!

The village shop sold jars of sweets and fizzy lollipops -
hand-made by Mr Walker- which made it King of shops
to all the village children, who obeyed the unwritten
rule -
'always call at 'Walker and Hall's' when you come out
of school.'

Next to the fridge stood jars of 'fizz'; crystals of yellow
and green -
2ozs of heaven in a triangular bag -
out of the shop we'd whiz,
to lie in fields behind a screen
of Hawthorn hedge and trees . . .

Hypnotised by clear blue skies
we drank our various pops,
like 'Dandelion and Burdock'
from bottles with impossible tops!

Easter was a special time in that dear old village shop -
with Easter eggs of every size,
but one that made eyes pop,
made from white sugar, it stood so proudly there.
An oval cut into the side, with flowers all around,
hid a tiny scene created inside with tender loving care.

I gazed in awe for several days,
I don't know where it went,
but in my heart it still remains - mine.
No one else could have imagined disappearing inside
and living with the characters.
It would have been so fine . . .!

VISUALIZATION

Fountain, mountain, meridian line;
imaginary journey
midst splendour so fine.

Acceptance, love, kindness;
enveloping cloak of blue
healing, holding, real and true.

Crystal peaks, coral comfort;
humility to renew.
Guardian spirits come to you.

Divinity; cascading golden light,
descending on despair.
A host of Angels show they care.

MY SPIRITUAL HOME

Pink mists of blossom
beside a tranquil stream.
Mystical, haunting music
- allowing me to dream
of pastures new . . .

Gossamer clouds with floating shrouds of white.
Pale blue healing sky, tinged with ethereal light;
backdrop to the scene
- allowing me to dream
of the dimension from whence I came . . .

Violet rays surrounding me - protecting me from reality;
softening earth's sharp, vicious blows
- allowing me to dream
of another land.
My Spiritual Home!

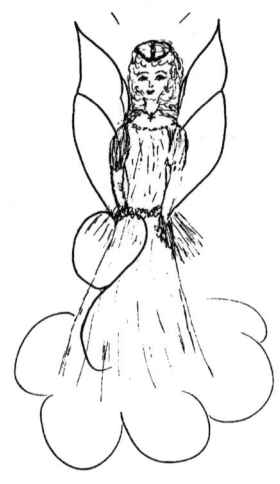

RELAX!

Happiness lights up the mind.
Our frontal lobe just longs to find
a breathing space - we just don't see -
that stopping thinking sets us free!

RECONNECT

When you snuggle down in bed at night
pray for dreams to make things right.
Get in touch with your 'inner-me'
and re-create your world to be
happy, loving, fun - and free!

LET GO!

When eyes are tired of peering
through a maze of pain and lies.
When hands begin to struggle
with knotted family ties.
When aching limbs and aching heart
bring heavy, weary sighs.
The higher-self reminds us
to rise above the cries
of earthly pain and weakness
- and all the desperate 'Why's?'
For when we feel most doubtful
it's the time to just 'let go'
and let our Guardian Angel
begin to run the show!

POWER OR STRENGTH

What is power - control of a life?
Confident, controlling, calculating knife
that cuts into pieces a life being led,
leaving behind a person who's bled
dry of all feelings, motivation and pride;
a sensitive someone who's quietly died -
leaving an outline, no soul left inside.

Is power strength - or is power obscene -
taking, destroying another's dream?
Will no one challenge the arrogant man
who oozes charm, as part of his plan
to dominate, dictate, demand or dismiss
any emotion which just isn't his!

Puffed up with pride he is carried along
by all of the 'yes' men who want to be 'strong'.
Their basic survival depends on his word
- no challenge, no comment; it's really absurd!
An air of authority; a bullying way -
mustn't be questioned, but maybe one day
man's inner-strength will whisper and say
'Stay true to yourself, it's better that way.'

Downtrodden, despairing, despondent or not -
who'd want the 'power' the other has got?
Strength, not power, comes from within,
not seeking glory, or desperate to win.
It patiently waits for the circus to end -
then strength can emerge, victorious again!

MR COOPER

The field looked so inviting, with flowers everywhere,
we wandered in through the old farm gate,
without a single care.
Three girls with summer holidays stretching out ahead -
one more day at school, then *'Freedom!'* we all said.

We were so busy practising for care-free days to come,
that we didn't see the grazing cows -
until they charged at us!
Through the hedge we scrambled, into a chicken run . . .
My long hair caught in the wire
- I was well and truly stuck -
when a cow butted my rear end -
Oh! What a piece of luck!
My yelling caused one friend to cry,
the other sat there - stunned -
when all at once we saw a man
with a twinkle in his eye . . .
'They only want to get to know you,'
he said, with quiet sigh.
With cheery chuckle he walked back to his door -
and left the three of us, still sitting on the floor!
With faces red we crept away -
the clump of hair clutched tight.
Harmless cows, innocent kids
and a man who saw our plight;
he was no threat - no price to pay -
for exploring on that sunny day!
A village set in peaceful times
when small things satisfied.
I can't help feeling a little sad that innocence has died.

CHOCOLATE TRUNKS

Chocolate flake tree trunks;
twisted branches aloft.
Winding walk through woodland
over earth cool and soft.

Occasional bird-song;
occasional sound,
but it's in the silence
that magic is found.

The past comes alive
in Nature's grand mast;
massive oak trees
their shadows now cast . . .

THE CRUEL SILENCE

No time to touch a shoulder -
or give a hand a squeeze,
with embarrassed sigh they hurry by
with no attempt to ease
the pain.
How much easier to dismiss or to shame
the bereaved into never mentioning the name
of those they see no more . . .

No time for reflection; no memory shared -
no comment to show that someone else cared
for the one you loved.
Just cold, empty faces, safe in their world
untouched by pain - fate's hand uncurled
caressing their face - not yet unfurled
the aching void of the lonely man's world.
The cruel silence.

ONE SKY

Prophetic messages in the blue light of dawn,
calm imposed on rosebud lawn.
Sacred, silent visions obliterated
by restrictions of the morn.

Hot airless tunnels reject the ghostly dance
of eloquent, simple pleas
scattered on the wind of chance
by voices on the sea.

The valley collects teardrops
shed by mountains
promising shelter from the fountains
of lies springing from barren ground.

JUNE

Whispering voices of busy birds,
a lilting saxophone tune;
shimmering heat - haze
and fresh green trees.
A perfect day in June.

THE PUREST FLAME

Candles of yellow to cheer us.
Candles of blue help us heal.
Candles of pink to surround us with love.
Candles of red? Instant zeal!

Candles of green bring balance
Candles of orange bring joy
- but candles of white,
with their soft glowing light
have the purest flame of them all!

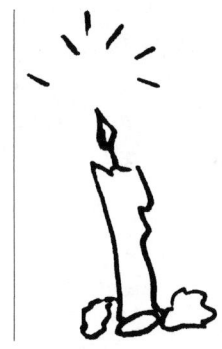

GRANDAD'S GARDEN

Secret garden of roses
tumbling over arches;
water spilling fountain
near garden seat
imposes.
The lilac and the willow tree,
laburnum and the larch
- bluebells, snowdrops, daffodils
peeping violets see
the wonder of the garden,
so loved by you and me.

Photos show the garden seat,
two smiling folk look on,
linking arms and laughing
- now sadly both are gone.
But somewhere in the garden
a Spirit quietly rests
and comes alive in bird-song
- still welcoming the guests!
Through winding paths and fox-gloves,
o'er grass of mossy green,
a gentle, laughing spirit
is heard - but never seen!

ANGELS OF LIGHT

Angels of light
will always bring
comfort to your soul.

Angels of love
will never let
another spoil your goal.

Angels of comfort
will bring you
peace inside your heart.

Angels of hope
will hug you today,
as you begin to make a new start . . .

BULLIED!

Oh lonely child you hide your fears -
keep inside the darts and spears
that tear you apart.
Inwardly dying; outwardly smiling - laughing face,
inside crying!
You feel worthless, a failure, a misfit - a thief;
stealing love, time - and in return
bringing pain.
Will they ever learn?

Misery is a cloak you wear, nothing takes away
the grief . . .
overwhelmed with despair you hide away -
only God knows what you have suffered that day!
I long to hold you, tell you 'be strong,
one day they'll know what they're doing is wrong!'
But you've closed down the hatches
- can't take any more,
will I ever see back the child of before?

And now as I hold you - your body a screen
I long to share with you all that you've seen . . .
our tears flow together, towards me you lean.
Inside our heads we silently scream.
Bullying! How obscene!

DESTINY!

Have faith that
when the time is right
all will be well.

Know that
when the time is right
you'll have the wisdom to tell.

Accept that
until then you may rest
safe in your shell.

The pathway now hidden
one day will be cleared
and nothing will be as bad as you feared!

BUTTERCUPS AND DAISIES

The black lead grate, ash pouring through the grid,
sung all night as winter hid
next year's flowers under snowy veil -
and the old man smiled as he told his tale.

With mother-of-pearl accordion always by his side
- hauntingly, magically, breathing in and out -
echoing the messages that he sang about.
His blue, twinkling eyes, his neat moustache of white,
showed a man with pride.

We all took a journey down the old railway-track,
where once he had been signal-man,
and now as he looked back
we pictured rambling roses, grasses waving tall,
brambles in the hedgerows - but most clearly of all -
we saw him pulling levers in the box along the line.

Old wooden steps linked his world
with the world of you and I
- steam trains hissed and whistled
as they all hurried by.
Hard-working hands made daisy-chains,
with buttercups for me.
Such treasured gifts, such tranquil days,
such a happy memory -
of days long gone, when as a child
Grandad G   I went to see . . .

ISN'T IT?

Isn't it strange what we believe
at different times in life?
Isn't it easy to misconceive
and cause heart-breaking strife?

Isn't it time we understood
another's point of view?
Isn't it love and compassion
that will surely see us through?

Isn't it sad that pride creeps in
and forgiveness is shown by few?
Isn't it time - after all this time -
to see 'judging' just will not do!

DREAM CATCHER

Over my bed is a delicate net,
woven from silky, coloured thread.
Its tiny glass beads
bright raindrops are
and the gems in the centre
shine like a star.
A magical spider's web,
it is there
to trap evil dreams
and keep me from care
- but the good dreams
it sprinkles down on my head
- so I dream wrapped in peace
in my soft, warm bed!

MY OTHER FAMILY

From alienation to acceptance
From desperation to love.
From lonely walk to happy dance.
From sinking low to rising above.
Who could ask for more?

To know your name
To see your face.
To hear your point of view.
To feel your warm embrace.
Who could ask for more?

So much pain and secrecy.
So many miles
'tween you and me.
So much misunderstanding,
Who could take much more?

Finally - a family,
Finally - someone like me.
Finally - I know 'my place!'
Finally - a familiar face.
I shall never ask for more . . .

GUARDIAN ANGELS

Guardian Angels are simply there,
to hold us when we kneel in prayer.
To give us love,
to keep us warm
- to shelter us from bitter storm
of words and actions,
harsh and worse;
to help remove vindictive curse.
And if you haven't met yours yet,
they're out there waiting
- you can bet!
Before you say, 'A likely tale!'
just give them chance;
they will not fail
to find a way through thorny trail,
but first you must take time to see
your Guardian Angel
- on bended knee!
It may seem an old-fashioned act,
to kneel and pray,
but it's a fact
that many heads may bend
'in prayer'
- but hearts remain detached,
like icy stare.
Angels can never be misled,
pray from the heart
- forget the head!

MY MYSTERY ROOM

I go to my mystery room when I feel in deep despair,
it never disappoints me, it's always waiting there.
It has a look of ancient times, a clock that stands so tall -
a big old-fashioned mirror, that hangs upon the wall.

It has a sense of gentleness and when I enter there,
I get a peaceful feeling - a feeling that is rare.
It envelops me; it lifts me; surrounds me like a cloud,
gives me strength, escape and love - I long to say aloud
'Come in with me share my room -
come share this peace with me . . .'

But I don't even whisper, I don't breathe a word
no steps do I take - it's really absurd.
I just close my eyes to enter my 'room',
my mind sees it there, it's quite clear.
It doesn't cost money, it's really unique -
something that's seemingly true.
If you're feeling sad, why not close your eyes too
and dream of a room that is special for you!

FRIENDSHIP

Friendship may be many things -
a thought, a word or deed.

Friendship can be anyones -
if they forget their greed.

Friendship that is given
may not be returned.

But from the very giving,
a lesson may be learned.

We learn the joy of knowing
that we have done our best.

And though our path is troubled -
our soul has stood the test.

KATH

The wind-up gramophone sang loudly
and with windows open wide
we laughed and sang together.
She was always by my side.

'There's a Cloud in My Valley of Sunshine'
echoed loud and clear - for everyone to hear!
As I sang with that lady
I forgot all my innermost fear . . .

She sat by a flaming fire,
with never-ending heat
and chided me for wearing
my wellies on wrong feet!

Throughout my childhood she welcomed me,
from school I cycled free . . .
On Sunday when she sat in church
she winked wickedly at me -
then sang as loudly as could be!

She was my friend; my family's friend,
now safely in God's care.
On very lonely nights I can almost see her there . . .
I'm sure I hear her laugh and say,
'Sing and be happy
- today's a new day . . .!'

ANOTHER WORLD

There is a land of love
way beyond the stars;
it touches us when we're in pain
and gives us strength
to live again.

Its love replaces earthly love,
when there's none to be found.
Its tender touch
then strokes our hair,
without a single sound.

If you're afraid,
or feel alone,
without a kindly smile,
relax and know that other world
is with you - all the while!

THE FOUNTAIN OF LOVE

There is a fountain of sparkling gold
awaiting us somewhere.
If only we could picture this
- instead of feeling care!

There is a fountain of laughter
somewhere inside each soul,
waiting for us to link with it
and once again feel whole!

There is a fountain of love
flowing over each and everyone,
as they walk the lonely path
when loved ones have passed on . . .

REJECTION!

So easy to whisper, to point and to sneer,
So easy to destroy, with a sniggering leer.
Rejection; so ugly, so cruel, so wrong!
Thank you rejection for making me *strong!*

LIFE'S JIGSAW

Pieces of all shapes and size;
colours of every hue.
Life's just one big puzzle
- made up of me and you!

Some pieces are old and rugged;
some are bright and new.
Some have lots of character
and some are funny too!

I take a look around me
at the puzzle where I sit
and realise I've always known
- I'm the piece that doesn't fit!

So I'll leave this puzzle as it is,
fort those who think it's fine.
I'll stay 'outside' - alone, but free
- until there's a puzzle that's right for me!

Although this puzzle appeals to some,
to others it does not.
One thing's for sure for all of us,
there's one small special slot!

And when the missing piece - that's me,
espies the missing spot,
I'll pack my bag and wave goodbye
and be there like a shot!

THE CAT AND THE CANDLE

The cat sat licking
as the candle glowed.
The fire flickered
- outside it snowed.

Falling silently on leafless tree
- across the moors and o'er the sea.
A silent sky secretly spied
on lonely figures, cold, outside.

In old grey coat, with little hope,
a lonely man is left to cope.
No candle or fire to keep *him* warm;
no purring cat - just cold, bleak storm.

The door-way filled with shoppers bright,
now is his shelter for the night.
He sits beneath dismissive gaze
forlorn; alone, within his maze.

And somewhere in his lonely world
a gentle memory is unfurled
of Christmas many years ago,
when he was loved and loved the snow.

His mind recalled a time of fun,
when his new world had just begun.
Now like the snow becoming slush
his grip on life is not worth much!

A passer-by looks scornfully
upon the man and fails to see
the gentle soul beneath the dirt
whose only crime is feeling hurt.

No cat or candle - or fire-side
to renew his will to live.
No welcome hug; no kindly word.
A life extinguished. How absurd!

THE WILLOW

Winding, twisted trunks;
separate, yet joined
by a weavy, tweedy stump
set in solid ground.

Wispy, green ribbons,
falling from the sky,
encircling seat below
with a whiskery, whispering sound.

Angry, warning alarm call,
from tiny wren on high,
making lots of noise
- yet not wanting to be found!

Sunlight sparkling; seeping through
hinting at autumn;
the year's going by.
Whistling winds; winter's around!

I'M NICE - NOT WEAK!

I'm nice - not weak -
I like to seek
the gentle paths in life.
That doesn't mean I can't be strong
- or that I dare not speak!

I enjoy the role of mother -
but I'm a person too
(and by the way perhaps it's time
we looked at me and you!)

I've given you the 'inner-me';
the light that made me shine,
but now it's time to re-light the flame
- reclaim what's really mine!

I'll start to live my life anew,
my energy I'll save for me.
With time I'll find my inner-self
I'm nice - not weak - you see!

WHY?

Unanswered questions;
existence, not life.
Years of torment;
of struggle and strife.
'What of the future?'
With heavy heart you sigh.
But here's a different way to think;
'Heaven knows
- and why!'

FRIENDSHIP

My dear friend you 'phoned, when all my world
was drear -
took away my gloom, my deep unhappy fear
that all was lost.
You gave me peace - breathing space to see
that humanity was not as bleak as I, with lonely
tear, believed it to be.
Your friendship stretched out to me,
and gave my mind tranquillity.
Your cheerful smile - a reality of hope,
which gave me peace and helped me cope.

And so I thank you dearest friend -
in my thoughts I quietly say,
'It really is a blessing to know not just today -
but yesterday, with memories of kind and thoughtful
ways,
and tomorrow's life unknown . . .
I have your friendship - value it - and send my
love today,
silently - with deep sincerity.
I think you understand the thanks I can't express
for your kind gifts of hope and gentleness.

WISHES

If wishes were wands
I'd wave them over you
and make the heartache go away
- just love and laughter
I'd renew . . .

ONE LEAF

It was just a tiny leaf
insignificant - and yet
that one small leaf on wedding gown
brings comfort - not regret . . .
I cannot tell the story
it belongs to Mum and me,
but in your eye perhaps you too
small memories can see . . .
It isn't grand schemes we recall
when someone we love has gone,
it's little angel touches
that help us to go on . . .
Our heart - mind opens daily
if we just take the time
and other hearts can link with ours,
love really is sublime!
It cannot be extinguished,
it's there throughout each day.
It's just a leaf that tells *me* so
- what's sent to *you* to say,
a loved ones love
remains the same
and will never pass away . . .

THE MAGIC TOUCH

A falling star of inspiration
from ultra violet ray,
fell to the earth, unlocked the door
and helped me find my way.

A cosmic source of energy,
unseen magic touch, released me
from the dreary grip
of earth's grim reality.

Passion and love, once dormant,
sparkled into life
and left behind the isolation.
I know I shall survive.

MEMORIES

Precious happy memories
of days of work and fun.
Laughing eyes and sunshine smile
to a new dimension gone.

The love once given still warms the heart
of those whose love is true
and every day in some small way
a spirit visits too.

It's just a glimpse, perhaps a joke,
told from friend to friend,
that brings a smile and for a while
a broken chain can mend . . .

DEATH

Death is but an open door,
through which a soul has passed.
It shouldn't make us sad or fear
that some things cannot last.

For death is a beginning;
a way of moving on.
It sounds so harsh and final,
when it's really just step one!

Of life that's everlasting;
of love that never dies.
of a sweeter richer lifetime
way beyond the skies!

For death just whispers to us.
that a soul who brightly shone,
has walked beyond the doorway
- ahead, but never 'gone' . . .

THE CLOAK OF LOVE

If knowledge is power
- is wisdom a deeper way of knowing?
If white light is perfection
- is the thread of life pure gold?

If a baby is linked to its mother
and a symbol of peace is a dove,
are we held by the Universe
- by unseen ethereal love?

If so it's a wonderful feeling,
to know that wherever we go
Love's invisible cloak is keeping us safe
from all that this world can throw!

THE ROMANY AND THE BURGLAR

One miserable Monday morning a Romany
crossed my path,
told me many wonderful things;
pierced my loneliness, released my smile,
sold me a charm
- and was arrested.

One bright Sunday evening a burglar entered
my garden shed,
brazenly smirked, gave me his name.
'No crime's been committed,' the policeman said.

The latter shattered my piece of mind,
The Romany's gentle, accurate, kind
words lifted me for a while.

Her crime! Selling the charm?
The burglar, with many convictions, doing such harm
walked free - smiling at me.
His eyes were steel; her gift was real.
I know which one I'd rather be!

COLOURFUL VIBRATIONS

Dragonfly; heart - hazed serenity,
tranquillity and gentleness.
Graceful grasses
'neath serene sky.
Peace and thankfulness.

THE UNENLIGHTENED

Glistening dew on angel wings
to the unenlightened
means not a thing.

Desperate prayers of victims
studiously ignored.
by the unenlightened.

Stories carried on the wind,
sacred tears of mountains
fall on the unenlightened.

Broken spirits, divided by fear;
ruled in ignorance
by the unenlightened.

Power, all consuming egos.
No escape for victims of greed
- the unenlightened.

FOXES AND FAWNS

Fairies and raindrops
foxes and fawns.
Frosty evening; freezing morn.
Fire-red berries
and cobwebs are worn
by leafless hedgerows;
spring yet unborn.

In white gown of crystal,
serene by the lake;
a wistful willow considers her fate.
Bare branches are hidden by frosty dawn;
angel dust scattered
by Nature's wise hand
- breathtaking beauty -
whilst resting the land . . .

YOU'RE NEVER ALONE

Seemingly endless nights
of lonely isolation
- where once love filled
each breath . . .

Silence greets each heavy sigh
- with no consolation
or simple reply
to all unanswered questions . . .

Memories merge, as tears escape
from sad, unseeing eyes
and through the darkness - way beyond
an angel hears the cries . . .

Love links us daily

WHY ME?

Do you ever wonder why it always seems
it is only you who can't fulfil your dreams?
Do you ever ponder on efforts gone unseen?
Do you ever look at those,
who though so cruel and mean,
seem somehow to reach their goals
through methods so unclean?

Do you ever look at them,
their smug, superior smiles -
then think about the way they feel
when they look around and see
the misery they've created
for folks like you and me?

Do you ever pause and say
'Let it go, it's not my way.'
Do you feel when sadness comes,
it will not stay-and rise above-
then thank God in his mercy
for blessing you with love!

THE WOODPECKER

The tap - tap - tap of cruel words
begin to break the one
who once loved life - was calm and strong.
No words of love, all kindness gone . . .

A rock now sandstone, crumbling away;
energy almost gone.
Faith, hope and love - tap, tap, tap . . .
so sad, so cruel, so wrong,
to break a spirit
that once was strong!

THE DIFFERENCE

Just a little break . . .
Just a change of pace . . .
Just a little kindness . . .
such a difference makes!

WELCOME HOME!

Closed eyes; closed soul.
Narrow eyes; narrow mind.
Open laughter; open smile.
Welcome arms; welcome home!

THE CALLER AT THE DOOR

When nights begin to darken
and days are not so warm,
as leaves begin to fall once more,
the victims of a storm
our homes become a sanctuary -
somewhere to hide away
and rest awhile
- to leave behind the troubles of the day.

For those who live alone
dark nights may endless be,
without a cheery word to help
from maybe you or me.
For some the saddest time may be
the coming of the fall -
dark nights the final curtain,
the loneliest time of all.

As we prepare for winter,
our plans already made,
let's spare a thought, a word or deed,
to give an hour to those who need
to see a friendly face -
a caller at the door.
When nights are long and cold and bleak
we're needed even more.

ETHEREAL STREAM

Lyrical sounds; whispering willows.
Images of fern and frothy lace,
of green and cream; a fairy face.
Magical, tranquil meeting place
of lovers through the years.
Tinkling, transparent pathway unfurled;
sparkling streams of liquid-sun
clear, delicate, delicious trail
of the life-blood of the world.
Uniting God, Spirit, Man . . .
A miracle since time began!

ANGELS

Angels visit every day,
each day our whole life through.
Angels quietly whisper
the things we shouldn't do.
Angels give us loving hugs
when life's too much to bear!
Angels always stay with us
when no one seems to care.
Angels are invisible
but Angels aren't a dream.
Angels are companions
whose love is never seen . . .

THE MAGPIE

I try to be magnanimous
but the magpie
and its chattering
seem to creep
deep within my inner-self;
it makes me want to weep.
It seems obsessed with power
over smaller, gentler birds.
Its presence seems to dominate,
with actions, more than words.
Perhaps its bullying nature
reminds me of
bitter aggression
- where once
there was love . . .

ESCAPE FROM THE LITTLE PEOPLE

Microscopic man;
mean-spirited
small.

Fragments in a nutshell
of a
nonentity.

Spirited, sparkling
laughing eyes;
despised.

By the little people
with no heart
- no mind!

Mean spirited; belittling
they play their part
gladly.

Destroying the joy
of the free spirit's
soul.

Chipping away.
The Spirit has gone.
- *Flown!*

JUDGE AND JURY

When women weep they weep alone;
menfolk scatter, or sit like stone.
Panic darting from their eyes
- staying silent to them seems wise.

And as the silence grows and grows
the aching chasm holds her woes
deep within its murky depths
- until a suitcase stands on steps,
where once a bride had stood . . .

She quietly leaves; she cannot stay
in a house that took away
her spirit, joy and sense of self.
They'll say she's leaving for more wealth
- instead of fighting for her health . . .!

If the story's truth be told
for twenty years her soul's felt cold.
And as it shrivels with the years
- wounded by the bitter spears
of heartless comments, senseless spite
a figure walks into the night . . .

A RAINDROP FELL

A raindrop fell,
it hit me in the eye.
I raised my fist and madly waved
at dark offending sky!

The thunder crashed and all its friends
cascaded on my head.
I stood wet through, then realised,
that little things should not be fed
by angry thoughts. I smiled instead.

And then I thought about my life,
the little niggles - giant strifes -
and realised with relief and glee
the big events aren't up to me!

Woven days of memories bright
are threaded through with cold, dark night.
And like the raindrop in my eye
- my little life's just passing by . . .

FREEDOM

Floating flowers; fleeting form;
flying pheasants; flawless fronds;
fluid fjords; flamboyant frogs.
Freedom found.

YOU AND ME

Your mind can be re-programmed,
just by using light.
Bombard the black spot on your soul
with gentle healing white.
Imagine rainbow colours
cascading over you.
Lilac, blue and lavender -
cream and cherry too.
Picture healing waters; sparkling, clear and blue.
Touch green grass and orange greet,
as rose-pink's love - with green complete -
now tumbles over you.
Never underestimate or forget to see
the power of colour
surrounding you and me . . .

THE TREE OF LIFE

Some days I'm an oak,
nothing will bend
the joy that I feel
or the love that I send.

Some days I'm a willow
swooping and swaying - flying quite free,
laughing at life
and just being me.

Some days I'm the holly
prickly to all,
standing alone - ignoring the call
of those who seem happy and jolly!

Today I have learnt
that more than just three
make up my life;
the tree that is me . . .!

HOME GOAL

E Mail and Internet?
How I long to be
back in the days
when 'internet'
meant football before tea!

OH HAPPY DAYS!

Washing machines and microwaves
answer machines and such.
Machines for this, machines for that.
I don't like them very much!

RAVING!

Garage or house?
Not even a mouse
would venture where
Rave music is playing.
They just wouldn't dare!

POLITICALLY CORRECT

Don't give me a hug?
Political correctness,
the modern day bug!

FALSE PRIDE

Majestic, elegant portraits hang - instilling fear;
drawn by paternalistic pen.
Ethereal sphere and hemisphere;
will 'o' the wisp men.
Greatness imagined.
Reality?
Dreary. Dull.
Self-important them
- 'though minuscule
in God's plan
of creating
a caring, humble man . . .

FROZEN GROUND

When fear freezes your very soul
and a step you cannot take.
Enjoy the rest, just take the space
to sit or lie . . . it's not a waste!

Frozen ground a seed will hold,
tightly, lonely, desperate, cold
until the morning of the spring
when once more free your soul will sing.

Life's gentle rain will ease the pain
with healing tears, then once again
the sun will give sweet comfort true.
Just take your time - it's good for you.

CRUSHED!

Pain and heartache side-lined
as heavy hands lash out.
Look of fear;
unfocused brain,
silent tear
- tension -
all consuming.
He's destroying you
- again!

CATCH THE DREAM

The dream is yours; it belongs to you.
Let no one take that dream,
destroy it, or break it in two.

Believe in yourself; let life unfold
and let no other's view
restrain, restrict or stifle
the Being that is you!

THE ETERNAL LIGHT

At times we may walk in shadows
but the heavenly light within
can never be extinguished
- the shadows will never win!

ONLY A CAT?

Independent. Eyes that see
right into your soul.
A winning way that is the key
to making you feel whole -
when all seems lost.

A healing stretch, contented yawn,
that lets you know the cat was born
to live a life of bliss!
With wary eyes and silent sigh
they blink, but never miss
the chance to comfort you.

When life brings fear and loneliness,
and no one else is there,
a little furry figure shows
what it really means to care!

Though some may scoff and never see
what it means to you and me
to feel close to 'only a cat'
I can't help but smile and quietly say
'They're certainly far more than that!'

GRANDFATHER OF THE FENS

Grandfather of the Fens has gone
far beyond his wildest dreams,
to another land.
Gnarled oak hands are still;
spirit as strong as the trunk
from which branches shed their magic
into tomorrows he will never own.

His Legacy

Yesterday's tranquillity and seeds of laughter sown
grow in desolation, peacefully, alone.
Wondrous glimpses here and there
of his spirit, everywhere.
A lilac tree, lilies small; gentle as he,
with kindly face, knew they would be.
Ageing roses set in a different time slowly unfurl
bringing sanity to an insane world!

His Legacy

Through the mists of memory
he walks the country lanes;
smiling, laughing, caring - quietly spreading joy.

Sharing thoughts, reliving times
he treasured as a boy.
Nature, his constant companion, flourishes;
- encouraged by his hand.
Faces smile at his memory,
as people tend their land
with happiness, love and pride;
an unseen, loving friend
is walking by their side.

His Legacy

SAFE ARMS

Oh gentle soul your sweet embrace
will always hold me near.
Your tender, all consuming love
protecting me from fear.

ANGELS OF THE DAWN

Emerald pyramids of memories
exploding in my head;
cascading fountains of laughter
- remembering things they said.

A clear crystal gown surrounding me,
protecting my body and soul;
enveloping love of the people
who once were my life now console . . .

Angel voices whisper their greetings,
trying so hard to be heard,
coming to me in the chorus
of the early morning bird.

Touching my face with fate's fingers
- gently caressing my pain,
holding me, content to linger
- until I'm at peace once again.

TOO LATE!

Smiling hand-in-hand through life,
the lucky people go.
Knowing strength and happiness
that some will never know.

No cruel words; impatient tongue,
or wanting so much to belong.
The 'chosen' ones, it sometimes seems,
are never meant to know sweet dreams!

Just pain and suffering
- every day -
and desperate cries
along their way.

Although they may accept their 'lot'
and understand another's tears,
they've been forgotten
through the years . . .

And when one day they cease to be
-unseeing eyes begin to see
the gift they tried so hard to share
so very precious; no longer there.

SEPTEMBER SLUMBERS

September slumbers - its smoky haze
o'er fields of stubble,
the sky ablaze
with golden, evening sun.
A touch of warmth, a cooling breeze,
spinneys of trees - no longer green
with the freshness of new life,
stand quietly by.
Gently rustling leaves
heave a weary sigh . . .

Soon autumn winds will strip them bare,
yet tall they'll stand - without a care.
When winter frosts have finally gone
and spring is at the door
with magic shake they will awake
refreshed; alive once more.
Resplendent trees, so wise, so strong,
renewing hope when all is wrong.
Relax and rest, be like the tree,
- and set your spirit free!

THE SPIRIT OF THE BIRD

Flight; the freedom of the soul
exploring sights unknown to man.
Soaring on unseen wings - whole -
completing God's plan.

Joy; the multitude of song
greeting another day -
each learning to survive
in their own special way.

Comfort; singing for the lonely,
surviving against great odds,
reminding us daily
that the master-plan is God's.

Faith; to remind us that our spirit
has brought us this far -
to lose faith now would be absurd.
Each day our soul possesses
the spirit of the bird!

MONA

Misty memories in a photo frame,
some sketches here and there.
A birthday book with covers closed
and inside by your name
a verse once written there.

The green silk cover's faded now,
with pages torn and thin,
loving comments, sometimes a vow,
to remember dates and friends . . .
Warmth radiates within.

And so it was when you were here
- 'though illness took its toll -
with twinkling eyes and loving ways,
sat by a fire of coal,
you quietly spent your days . . .

You've left this earth, I know it's true,
but many things still speak of you;
the words you said, the hugs we'd share,
embroidered cushions on a chair.
The words 'God Bless'; your cheery ways
still help me through my darker days . . .!

EVERLASTING LOVE

Fountains flowing; crystal clear water.
Splashing lonely tears
spill from eyes of pain.

Glazed, dazed; unseeing.
Tears the only respite
in days of cloud and rain.

Sweet serenity, your knowing eyes
are looking down on me,
bidding me to rise above
the pain and misery.

Willing me to seek new friends
- find joy and sanctuary . . .
and dare to be
just *'Me'*.

DAISIES

Daisies are amazing;
they suddenly appear
from soggy grass
'neath muddy boots.
They grow year after year.

The grass is cut;
they disappear
- or so we might believe.
Then there they are, alive and bright,
surviving through the year.

They are not known for status
as they quietly grow and live.
They are not there for grand display.
Would life not be much richer
- if we lived the daisy's way?

Close to the ground
but pure as light,
a heart of gold within.
Now what could be more right?

TOMORROW

Tomorrow might be heaven;
tomorrow might be hell!

Tomorrow might mean laughter
- or a sorry tale to tell.

Tomorrow might embrace us
- or snatch our joy away.

Let's forget about tomorrow
- just do our best today!

THE LINCOLNSHIRE BLACKBIRD

You visit each morning, swooping so low -
singing your song to let me know
I am not alone.

I watch from my window, the old lilac tree
provides a platform, you sing just for me.
I am not alone.

The field beyond is coming alive,
I count your companions - now there are five.
I am not alone.

Winter is passing, the berries all gone.
The Lincolnshire landscape all blending in one.
I hear your song.
I am not alone.

New life appears, your offspring emerge -
hopping and stumbling along the grass verge.
I am not alone.

Now swallows are building - there's other birds too -
you seem so joyful, there's none quite like you,
I am not alone.

I am not alone in this Lincolnshire fen,
'though one day you'll leave, I wonder when?
Today is the day;
I am alone.

INSPIRATION

What gives us the ideas to do the things we do?
What helps us make the effort to tackle something new?

What provides the strength to carry on and see a project
through?
What says it's time to share a new idea or two?

What is the word that we all need, but very rarely say?
The word is 'inspiration', it helps us every day!

LONELINESS

What do we mean by loneliness -
is it a state of mind?
Do we think that loneliness
makes it hard to find
a friend to listen, a friend to care -
or a husband or wife, who cannot be there?

What do we mean by loneliness?
Being with others, yet feeling alone -
part of us talking and laughing aloud -
the other part feeling left out from the crowd?

What do we mean by 'being aware'
could it be giving and showing we care?
Taking the time to hold someone near,
quietly taking away their fear
of loneliness . . .

FATE

Are heavy boots of negativity
dragging you down?
Or dancing shoes of creativity
taking you to town?

Depressing sigh of resignation
- or gleeful, happy smile -
what is your destination?
Quietly sit there for a while . . .

And as you ponder
on life's troubles
- your heart a stone within -
very slowly cheerful bubbles
will remind you how to grin . . .

Fate may have decided
that your path
is craggy rock and hole
- that several stumbles are required -
before you reach your goal!

THE DANCE OF LIFE

Twirling, whirling - full of joy -
dancing, prancing - never coy!

Rushing, pushing - charging through -
huge feet stamping over you!

Tinkling, twinkling fairy dance
lightly flitting - Prance! Prance! Prance!

Different dances, different days;
different paces, different ways.

The Dance of Life brings many things
- Adjust your step and cut the strings.

Whichever dance you choose to do,
don't be a puppet - just dance for you!

ATTITUDE

We cannot change events in life -
but attitude can be the knife
that cuts through endless pain
and gives us strength
to live again!

THE VISITOR

Journey's end is just the beginning,
people to visit,
lives to touch -
worlds to cross and laughter to bring.
Mysteries to create by the magic of the soul
travelling on unseen rainbows
into other people's lives.

Electric atmosphere; lights that dazzle - dim -
then dazzle again
TVs that click and channels that change
inexplicably . . .
A golden butterfly is lifted from the Christmas tree;
fluttering against the window-pane, miraculously alive,
a brightly coloured friend appears;
a symbol of hope.
The snow falls silently.

I am the soul that is the click; the flutter, the light that
shines.
I am invisible, but I am here -
a phoenix risen from the ashes of yesterday
to bring joy tomorrow.
I know this house well; it knows me.
The cat's eyes are my eyes; her mistress understands.
She looks into my eyes - feels reassured and safe.
The cat stretches, contentment is hers
and mine.

I am spirit, travelling between two worlds;
an unseen being of light
crossing the 'Bridge of Life' for an instant today,
tomorrow and for eternity.
A reminder of times that weren't quite as lonely . . .
I wish only to share my happiness with those I loved -
and who loved me.
I am no strange force to be feared.
Light is love; love is light.
Love is eternal.
I am love.

GENTLENESS

Whatever happened to gentleness -
when did it disappear?
Where is it hiding; why do we see
less of it every year?

What ever happened to words such as care -
where did the plan go astray?
How did it become unpopular to share -
to stop giving our time away?

Who will be 'brave' and no longer need
all of the things we 'should' have -
step off the treadmill of wanting and greed,
take the time for a joke and a laugh.

New values; new interests - unimpressive to some -
may be what's needed in the century to come.
Renew the art of chatting, restore our spirit too.
Perhaps it's almost time to change our point of view.

Together we can look at life the way we used to do
before we got entangled in living
as others said we should -
if we wanted to 'succeed' have 'power' and look good . .

We'll walk along a hidden track and take the time to see
wildlife, hedges, flowers - left by Nature's loving hand.
We'll look again at what God meant
when he visualised our land.

And when at last we're homeward bound
we'll smile and quietly say,
'I think I nearly caught a glimpse
of gentleness
today . . .'

It's not just a word, but a way of life;
away from walking the edge of a knife.
Hidden away like the overgrown track -
peace of mind is unfolding - it's finally coming back.

BITTERNESS

Bitterness destroys the soul; the being that is you -
it brings consuming pain
colouring all you do.

It takes a mind that started out with love and hope
and pride
and turns it upside down -
turmoil that's hard to hide.

If bitterness becomes your friend - beware -
for on that day
God's plan for you will slowly slip away.
So shed your bitter tears, let them fall as they may
but even on the saddest day
make bitterness leave - go right away!

Instead, let out the jumbled pain
that drives your mind insane -
then begin to smile and realise
that life comes right again.
'Bitterness' - say the word aloud -
hear the way it sounds; hard, unfeeling, full of hate.
Your life deserves a better fate!

YOU

You are a mystery to him -
yourself - a dream!
Unreal, pretending - you - a theme.
Assertive, quiet, introvert -
giving love unseen . . .

You are being 'selfish' now . . .
considering your own needs . . .
Not giving all you've got to him -
a woman moving on.
When *He* moves that is progress,
but a feminist is strange -
doesn't belong.

Funny how being 'you' is suddenly so wrong!

AT LAST!

Why? Why am I here,
awaiting gentle love's embrace;
knowing all that life will give
is pain inside this space,
known as 'home'?

Where? Where is the smile
lighting up a face,
wanting to be supportive of me,
when pain invades
my space?

How? How do I find love
that knows no cruelty,
or harsh impatience aimed at me;
disturbing, not appreciating home
- or me?

When? When the time is right,
then I shall know.
Quietly, softly I shall leave;
when no-one's there to see me go,
- happily seeking my Spiritual home.

GOD'S LIGHT

Effulgent; effusive; resplendent; free.
God's light forever shines in me.
Its essence within;
insurmountable, invincible - no fantasy -
the vital spark that no one can see.

Forever safe through the vicissitudes of life.
Its perception of radiance - ignoring strife -
resplendent, 'though unseen vision,
beyond pure white light . . .
Incandescent radiance;
bright day, after long, dark night.
God's angels share each day with me.

A GLIMMER OF HOPE

Crumbling spirit cascades
into nothingness.
Life's essence
now just a bleak glimpse
of sadness;
a tear on cheek.
Suitcase in hand,
awaiting the flame
of freedom to call
and ignite the candle
asleep in us all . . .

UNCONDITIONAL LOVE

I gave my love to you - unconditionally.
I really thought you felt the same
- your love was there for me.
But on the stormy nights I found
somehow your love was not around . . .

Life's bitter blows had changed you
to someone I didn't know;
from kindred spirits to strangers.
- how could this be so?

A life-long love had slowly died,
just emptiness - a void inside -
where once you'd dwelt in me.

I really wish that I could feel
the love I used to feel,
but all the pain has made me feel
beaten, dejected and unreal.

Now, at last, I began to see
a way I can survive;
I'll love myself, instead of you.
- unconditionally . . .!

MAGICAL MOMENTS

Wings of white
surround my soul;
physical world,
that makes me whole,
diminishes in importance
as my spirit brings
glimmering glimpses
of beautiful things . . .

Colourful insights
of blue and gold
other-worldly
- beautiful, bold . . .
Magical movements
of wavering sea;
God-given moments
sent 'specially for me!

WORDS

How difficult to say the words
that fill our hearts and mind.
How many times we 'mean' to say
- but don't - or maybe find,
that somehow we are pressured,
our lives just hurry by,
and things are left unsaid
that could help a lonely cry.

Perhaps if we could take the time
to realise and see
that *saying* words not *thinking* them -
really is the key.
Then as we journey on our way -
and others journey too -
those words may mean that life for some
has meaning that is new . . .

MARK

You are what you always were;
a lovely spirit
free.
With laughing eyes and sunshine smile
you walk each step with me.

As I lie awake before the break of day,
I smile at happy memories
and funny things you'd say.
I quietly reminisce
about the hidden part of you,
which I especially miss;
the loving hugs, the caring side so true.
I touch your gifts, look at your photos too.

And through the aching sadness,
I know there'll always be
a truly happy spirit forever here with me.
For love knows no divide,
there's no such thing you see -
you are the same as you always were
a lovely spirit
Free!

THE HAPPY ME

The Happy Me feels the sun's warmth
and sees the stars at night.

The Happy Me walks by a stream
that wanders through a tranquil scene.

The Happy Me smells creosote logs
burning on an open fire

The Happy Me laughs with friends
whose laughter can inspire.

The Happy Me likes simple things
- enjoys the peace contentment brings.

The Happy Me is a golden thread
woven into my body and soul

The Happy Me is a bright, white light
which shines even on the darkest night.

The Happy Me is a silver, fleeting form
flowing with the river to the sea.

The 'Happy Me' remains the key
that allows us to be what we were born to be -
Happy!

ALWAYS

Although life may not bring
all you thought it might bring;
although there are times when the 'phone doesn't ring,
although there are times when you almost despair . . .
Always remember that someone is there.

THE FINAL JOURNEY

Floating garments of violet
support my soul;
Earth's chains no longer hold me
as I gently journey home,
on wings of light.

From tear-stained eyes
to paradise
From earthly pain
to love.
From cruel world
to sweet caress.
From bitter words
to words that bless . . .
on wings of hope.

Freedom; perfect freedom,
is calling my name.
Freedom; perfect freedom,
extinguishing the flame.
Heraldic wings of joy . . .
Mine!

THE INNER SELF

The windows may have cobwebs,
but when the sun shines through
the inner room may delight you
with a very different view!

Although outer walls have crumbled
with the passages of time,
the cosy warmth - and clock with friendly chime -
are always there to welcome you . . .

And so it is with people - look beyond the frame -
the inner-self might be aglow,
calling out your name.
So beautiful; so spiritual - more perfect than the mind.
Let's not forget the part of us that cannot be defined.
For as we strive for 'greater' things,
we forget the gift our Spirit brings!

LITTLE PEOPLE

Little people, little minds -
scheming ways to score.
Little people, bitter tongues.
Weren't we born for more?

THE SCHOOL NATIVITY PLAY

A robin swoops from the wings
with tiny gift in hand.
A child shouts from the audience,
'*Look! Look!* It's *Superman!*
The robin, quite indignant,
now forgets his lines.
The teacher quietly coaches
through paper-mache pines!

Mary's looking doubtful.
Jesus is in the crib.
Joseph looks at Mary and digs her in the rib.
The Wise Men start to argue
- no 'peace to all men'
as they begin to fight.
The inn-keeper's got a touch of flu,
- he cannot sing tonight.

Mothers sing 'While Shepherds Watched'
fathers stand quietly by, then look aghast
as, loudly, a baby starts to cry!
And yet the night is special
('though no one's certain why)
Perhaps God is gently touching us
with his healing hand, and through the children
whispering 'Peace throughout the Land.'

RAVING AT CHRISTMAS

Thud! Thud! Thud! It's eight o'clock,
the torture has begun!
My daughter's getting ready
to go out having fun.

Vibrating room; vibrating house!
The music (should I really call it that?)
has driven out a shaking mouse,
next to a trembling cat!

Her father's frown has deepened -
he's got the whisky out!
Bring back the days of 'The Beatles'
I long to 'Twist and Shout!'

JUST ANOTHER MUM

I've shopped and cooked.
I've trimmed the tree.
I've packed presents by the score.
I've written cards and posted them.
I've delivered even more!
I've bathed the kids.
I've visited Gran.
I've made the Christmas pud!
I've even iced the cake.
I've finished laying the table.
I've staggered for a bath.
I've just heard the words, 'Enjoying yourself?'
Now isn't *that* a laugh!

ESCAPE

I suppose we should feel happy
rushing here and there,
instead our nerves are frazzled
and there is snapping everywhere!

The dog has chased the cat again,
the twins have both been sick.
Auntie Glen has disappeared
and Jane's run off with Mick!

Peter's lost his marbles
and Paul's lost his lens - again!
Josh has written on the wall
with a giant marker pen.

Tim is 'phoning Australia
but I no longer care.
I've packed my bags and sun-tan cream.
I'm getting out of here.

IT'S ME TIME!

I've made a resolution
to consider my own needs.
I'm really going to start trying
keeping one or two seeds
of the wisdom I keep planting
for others every day!
I'm finally beginning to see
it's really not a crime,
to consider myself
- instead of others all the time!

CHRISTMAS

Carol's got a headache.
Henry's feeling cursed.
Rita's cooking turkey.
Ian's being nursed.
Susan's pulling crackers.
Tom has got a thirst.
Mandy's shaking presents
Andrew things he'll burst!
Successful Christmas! That would be a first!

PEACE AT CHRISTMAS

Snowflakes, white perfection.
Our Lady gazes down.
Sweet smile of serenity,
casting gentle eyes
o'er village, city, town . . .

With grace she listens quiet prayer.
With joy she offers love.
With silent tear she listens fear
- sends silently a dove . . .

As Pilgrims light a candle
and pray for joy, not pain.
Our Lady holds them in her arms
and souls find peace again.